ANIMALS ON THE BRINK
Giraffes

E. Melanie Watt

www.av2books.com

AV² provides enriched content that supplements and complements this book. Weigl's AV² books strive to create inspired learning and engage young minds in a total learning experience.

Your AV² Media Enhanced books come alive with...

Audio
Listen to sections of the book read aloud.

Key Words
Study vocabulary, and complete a matching word activity.

Video
Watch informative video clips.

Quizzes
Test your knowledge.

Embedded Weblinks
Gain additional information for research.

Slide Show
View images and captions, and prepare a presentation.

Try This!
Complete activities and hands-on experiments.

... and much, much more!

Go to **www.av2books.com**, and enter this book's unique code.

BOOK CODE

F 1 6 8 6 8 6

AV² by Weigl brings you media enhanced books that support active learning.

Published by AV² by Weigl
350 5th Avenue, 59th Floor
New York, NY 10118
Websites: www.av2books.com   www.weigl.com

Library of Congress Control Number: 2013953038

ISBN 978-1-4896-0564-1 (hardcover)
ISBN 978-1-4896-0565-8 (softcover)
ISBN 978-1-4896-0566-5 (single-user eBook)
ISBN 978-1-4896-0567-2 (multi-user eBook)

Printed in the United States of America in North Mankato, Minnesota
1 2 3 4 5 6 7 8 9 17 16 15 14 13

122013
WEP301113

Project Coordinator Aaron Carr
Design Mandy Christiansen

Contents

The Giraffe

What do you know about giraffes? You may know many facts already. For example, you may know that giraffes are very tall. In fact, giraffes are the tallest land animal in the world. This book will tell you how being tall helps the giraffe eat food and defend itself from harm. You will also learn how being tall makes it difficult for giraffes to take a drink of water or lie down. As you will discover, the giraffe's body is unique in many ways, from its hoofs to its horns to the end of its tail.

You may also know that a giraffe has an unusually long neck. Do you think this means it has more neck bones than you do? Read on to discover the answer. You will also find out what it means when two giraffes are **necking**, why giraffes' tongues are purple, and why giraffes whistle. You will learn which animals prey on giraffes and how giraffes help birds called oxpeckers. Turn the page and get ready to learn about the amazing giraffe, inside and out.

Giraffes live in groups across the plains of Central Africa.

How to Take a Stand on an Issue

Research is important to the study of any scientific field. When scientists choose a subject to study, they must conduct research to ensure they have a thorough understanding of the topic. They ask questions about the subject and then search for answers. Sometimes, however, there is no clear answer to a question. In these cases, scientists must use the information they have to form a hypothesis, or theory. They must take a stand on one side of an issue or the other. Follow the process below for each Take a Stand section in this book to determine where you stand on these issues.

1. **What is the Issue?**
   a. Determine a research subject, and form a general question about the subject.

2. **Form a Hypothesis**
   a. Search at the library and online for sources of information on the subject.
   b. Conduct basic research on the subject to narrow down the general question.
   c. Form a hypothesis on the subject based on research to this point.
   d. Make predictions based on the hypothesis. What are the expected results?

3. **Research the Issue**
   a. Conduct extensive research using a variety of sources, including books, scientific journals, and reliable websites.
   b. Collect data on the issue and take notes on all information gathered from research.
   c. Draw conclusions based on the information collected.

4. **Conclusion**
   a. Explain the research findings.
   b. Was the hypothesis proved or disproved?

A giraffe's neck and head can weigh 500 pounds (225 kilograms).

Giraffe
Facts

A giraffe's purple tongue reflects **ultraviolet** light from the Sun. This protects the tongue from sunburn.

A short mane grows along the back of the giraffe's neck.

Features

Giraffes are almost never mistaken for other animals. They have many unique features. These features include the giraffe's long neck and legs, large size, and special color pattern. A giraffe also has two or more hornlike growths on its head. Both males and females have horns, but females' horns are smaller and thinner than those of males. A giraffe's large, dark brown eyes have long lashes. The giraffe has large, heavy feet with hoofs. Each hoof has two toes. The animal's long, narrow tail ends in a tuft of hair.

Just how tall is a giraffe? Bulls, or male giraffes, are larger than cows, or female giraffes. The average height for bulls is about 17 feet (5.2 meters). For cows, the average height is 14 feet (4.3 m). The tallest giraffe ever recorded was a 19.3-foot (5.9-m) tall bull. By tilting its head up and sticking out its tongue, a giraffe can add an extra 3.5 feet (1.1 m) to its reach. Even young giraffes are big. At birth, they are about 6 feet (1.8 m) tall and weigh more than 220 pounds (100 kg).

Adult male giraffes are often heavier than adult females. An adult male usually weighs between 1,760 and 4,250 pounds (800 and 1,930 kg). An adult female usually weighs between 1,210 and 2,600 pounds (550 and 1,180 kg). Adult giraffes' tails are about 27 to 40 inches (69 to 102 centimeters) long.

Giraffes have very thick skins. Their hides can be up to 0.6 inches (15 millimeters) thick on their shoulders and are about 0.3 inches (7.5 mm) thick on their necks. Thick skin may help protect giraffes from parasites, or it may just be natural for an animal this large. The muscles attached to the giraffe's skin are not well developed. This makes it difficult for a giraffe to jiggle its skin, as a horse does, to shake off flies and other pests.

The giraffe's skin has patterns of light to dark brown markings on a cream-colored background. The brown markings can get darker with age. The skin on the underparts of a giraffe is usually light and unmarked. Each giraffe's pattern is unique. This pattern can be used, like human fingerprints, to tell individual giraffes apart. A giraffe keeps its pattern for life.

Although they are not common, there are white giraffes. There are also giraffes that are almost black. A few giraffes are completely tan colored, with no creamy background.

Classification

Giraffes are now found only in Africa, but their ancestors probably lived in Asia and Europe as well. *Prolibytherium* and *Zarafa*, two ancestors of the giraffe, lived about 25 million years ago. *Sivatherium*, a more recent ancestor, lived in Africa and Asia 5 million years ago. *Sivatherium* had a heavy build and stood 16 feet (4.9 m) tall.

Scientists group giraffes with other animals that have an even number of toes on their hoofs. These animals include pigs, camels, deer, hippopotamuses, antelopes, cattle, goats, sheep, and okapis. The okapi is the giraffe's closest living relative. Okapis live in forested areas of Central Africa. Like giraffes, okapis have very long tongues, which help them gather food.

All giraffes belong to one **species**. Scientists use the Latin name *Giraffa camelopardalis* for this species. It includes several types, or subspecies, of giraffes.

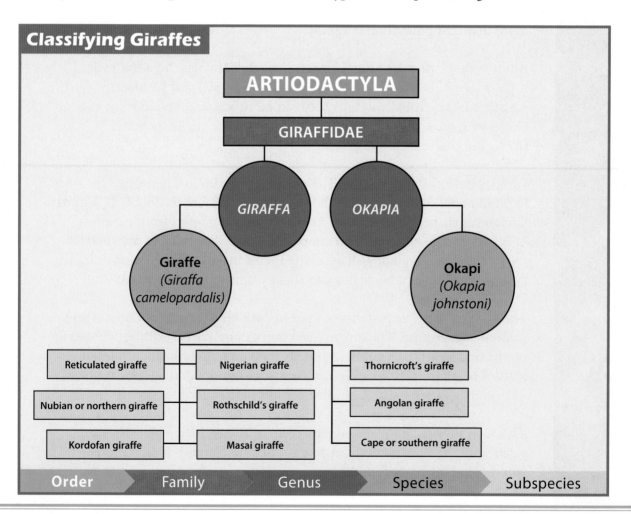

Classifying Giraffes

ARTIODACTYLA

GIRAFFIDAE

GIRAFFA — OKAPIA

Giraffe (*Giraffa camelopardalis*) — Okapi (*Okapia johnstoni*)

- Reticulated giraffe
- Nubian or northern giraffe
- Kordofan giraffe
- Nigerian giraffe
- Rothschild's giraffe
- Masai giraffe
- Thornicroft's giraffe
- Angolan giraffe
- Cape or southern giraffe

Order → Family → Genus → Species → Subspecies

It is easy to see where tall animals such as giraffes have been browsing, or eating from a tree. A "browse line" separates the top part of the tree, where the leaves are still growing, from the bare, lower sections.

Okapis can grow to about 5.5 feet (1.7 m) tall. They weigh about 700 pounds (320 kg).

The color pattern of some giraffes has broad patches. On other giraffes, the patches are smaller.

Special Adaptations

Giraffes have many special **adaptations**. These features help them survive challenges in their environment.

Tongue and Lips

The giraffe has a long, flexible tongue that it uses to pull leaves from trees. Its tongue is about 18 inches (45 cm) long. The tongue and lips are **prehensile** to help a giraffe pluck leaves. A giraffe's favorite leaves are from the acacia tree, which has many thorns and rough branches. To protect a giraffe's face when the animal is eating, the giraffe's lips are covered with hair.

Eyes

Giraffes have sharp eyesight. Their eyesight and their height allow giraffes to see farther than other land **mammals** can. They have been reported to be able to see a person 1 mile (1.6 kilometers) away. Giraffes use their good vision to help protect themselves against **predators**. Lions and other predators are more likely to attack when they can surprise their prey. Often, if a group of giraffes sees a lion approaching, they will stand facing the lion with their heads up. A watchful group of giraffes is not an easy target.

Lungs

A giraffe has huge lungs. They are needed to move used air all the way up its long neck and out when the giraffe exhales. Inside a giraffe's neck is a windpipe. It moves fresh air from the giraffe's nose and mouth to its lungs.

Horns

The horns on a giraffe's head are not true horns. They are made of bone and are covered with skin and hair. Horns on many other animals are covered with a material similar to human fingernails. The tops of the giraffe's horns are rounded, not sharp. Males use them to fight each other. The horns can be up to 9 inches (23 cm) long and 6 inches (15 cm) around. A giraffe may also have a knoblike structure between its eyes. This is called the median horn. When giraffes are born, their horns are made out of **cartilage**. As the horns grow, bone replaces the cartilage.

Neck

The giraffe uses its long neck to reach food found high in the treetops. Like most mammals, the giraffe has seven vertebrae, or neck bones. The giraffe's vertebrae, however, are much longer than those of other mammals. An adult giraffe's neck is about 6 feet (1.8 m) long. Strong neck muscles support the heavy bones. Joints on the back of its head allow a giraffe to raise its head straight up. This flexibility lets it reach leaves high on a tree.

Heart

A giraffe's heart is more than twice as big as scientists would expect for an animal of its size. The heart must be powerful to pump blood up to the animal's raised head. A giraffe's heart is about 2 feet (0.6 m) long and weighs about 25 pounds (11.3 kg).

Giraffe Facts

Giraffes are good jumpers. However, with their long legs and necks, they do not often need to jump to move around or reach food.

Giraffes can live to be more than 30 years old in captivity. In nature, they rarely live longer than 25 years.

Groups

Giraffes are often found alone or in pairs, but they also form herds. In herds, many individuals can be on the lookout for predators at the same time. An adult giraffe sometimes leaves its herd and then joins it again later. Adult male giraffes tend to travel alone, looking for females to mate with. Females and young giraffes usually stay together in a herd. When a female is found alone, she is often pregnant and has moved away from a herd to give birth.

Giraffes form herds of many different sizes. Pairs or small herds of giraffes are more common than large herds. Large herds of up to 154 giraffes were reported in 1868, before people began to destroy the giraffe's natural **habitat**.

When they are about 15 months old, male giraffes leave their mothers.

Young giraffes may moo or bleat when they are left alone.

Animals on the Brink

Communication

For many years, people thought giraffes could not make any vocal sounds. Although they are usually silent, giraffes do make a variety of sounds. Female giraffes may whistle to call their young. They may also make a roaring bellow.

A startled, angry, or hungry giraffe may grunt or snort. Giraffes may also grunt or snort to warn others in the herd of danger, such as a predator. Male giraffes sometimes make a coughing sound during mating. Giraffes living in zoos may bellow when they are hungry. Giraffes have also been reported to moan, growl, scream, sneeze, hiss, snore, and make a flutelike sound.

Scientists have recently discovered that giraffes also produce low-frequency sounds, which are too low to be heard by humans. Low-frequency sounds travel well across grassland areas in which many giraffes live. Scientists believe low-frequency sounds are produced when giraffes throw their necks and heads back over their bodies in a neck stretch. They may also be produced when a giraffe moves its head straight up. These movements may change how air moves up a giraffe's windpipe.

From an Expert

"The giraffe is not only physically but also socially aloof, forming no lasting bonds with its fellows and associating in the most casual way with other individuals whose ranges overlap its own."
Richard Despard Estes

Richard Despard Estes has studied many large African mammals and has written a book about their behavior. He leads photo safaris in Etosha National Park in northern Namibia. He has worked for the World Conservation Union, the Harvard Museum of Natural History, and the Smithsonian Conservation and Research Center.

Body Language

Although they can make many sounds, giraffes tend to be quiet animals. This is true even during most social interactions. Giraffes often communicate with each other by body movements.

Touching

A giraffe may use its nose to touch another giraffe on the body, neck, or head. Giraffes sometimes rub their heads on one another's body or neck. Standing giraffes will sometimes rub their legs against the back of a giraffe that is lying down. A female giraffe will touch its calf to guide it to food. Giraffes may also warn each other about predators and other dangers by touching.

Licking

A giraffe may lick another giraffe's body, neck, mane, or horns. A female giraffe licks her baby to reassure and clean it. Licking and touching may help giraffes form bonds with each other. For example, when a newborn giraffe joins a herd for the first time, the other adults nose the youngster.

Dominating and Submitting

A giraffe will threaten another giraffe or show **dominance** by standing up straight with its chin and head held high. It may also show that it is a threat by stretching out its neck and walking with stiff legs toward an animal or human. A giraffe that is defending itself or is showing that it is **submissive** to another giraffe will lower its head and ears. It will jump away and leave an area when the other giraffe approaches.

Running

Giraffes may communicate danger by running away. Often, the other members of the herd will stampede, or rush away, before they even know what the danger is. Giraffes walk differently than they run. When giraffes walk, they put all their weight on their left legs first and then on their right legs. When they gallop, they move their back legs as a pair and their front legs as a pair.

•Debate•
Take a Stand
•Research•

Does keeping giraffes in African reserves really help them?

Many giraffes in Africa now live on reserves, which are areas of land set aside for animals. Reserves protect giraffes and their habitat, but they also create problems. For example, acacia trees produce **tannins**. Giraffes are not harmed by low levels of these poisons. Acacias that are constantly eaten in reserves, however, produce more tannins, which may weaken giraffes.

FOR

1. Keeping giraffes in reserves helps protect them from **poachers**. Guards at the reserves help to stop illegal shooting.
2. Giraffes in reserves do not eat farmers' crops. Farmers sometimes shoot giraffes that feed on their crops.

AGAINST

1. Confining giraffes to reserves does not allow them to mate with giraffes outside their own area. Health problems within giraffe groups are passed down to future generations.
2. Reserves do not allow giraffes to roam as far as they naturally would to find acacia trees and other sources of food.

Giraffe
Facts

Giraffes are one of the only animals born with horns.

Baby giraffes nurse twice each day. A newborn can drink up to 1 gallon (3.8 liters) of milk at each feeding.

Mating and Birth

A female giraffe comes into **heat** for one day every two weeks until she becomes pregnant. This is the only time that she will allow a male to mate with her. Adult bull giraffes travel alone from herd to herd in search of a female in heat. Males may begin mating when they are about 3.5 years old, but most are much older when they mate for the first time. Young males are prevented from mating by older, larger bulls, who chase them away from cows in heat.

Females can become pregnant for the first time when they are about 3.5 years old. The **gestation period** for giraffes is about 15 months. Young giraffes are called calves. A female giraffe gives birth to her first calf when she is about 5 years old. She will then have others about every 20 months.

A female giraffe can become pregnant a few months after giving birth. Some mammals cannot easily become pregnant while **nursing**. Giraffes, however, can get pregnant while they are nursing. A female can produce calves until she is about 20 years old and may have as many as 10 calves in her lifetime.

Mother giraffes give birth in "calving grounds." Female giraffes in a herd often give birth around the same time. A giraffe will return to the same calving ground where she was born to have her baby. A female giraffe usually gives birth to and raises one calf at a time. Sometimes, giraffes have twins, but this does not happen often. A calf will start to nurse about one hour after standing.

A calf may be able to stand on its wobbly legs as soon as 20 minutes after it is born.

Calves

A mother giraffe keeps her newborn calf alone with her for the first weeks of its life. Mothers can be very protective of their young. They usually remain no more than about 80 feet (25 m) away from their calves during this time. They have been known to charge at people and predators to protect their newborns. Giraffe mothers even keep other giraffes away from their calves during these first few weeks.

Calves are vulnerable to predators. For the first few weeks of life, calves spend half of the day and most of the night lying hidden. When a calf is frightened, it lowers its head, which helps it hide. Scientists think that the calf's spotted coat also helps it blend in with its surroundings, hiding it from predators.

By the time the calf is 1 month old, the mother allows it to play with other young giraffes. It can also be near older giraffes. Groups of calves, called creche groups, are sometimes left with one or more adult females. They watch over the young so the other mothers may travel in search of food or water.

After the first 6 weeks of life, a calf may be away from its mother for many hours. Calves can go without nursing for long periods once they reach this age. Giraffe milk has about three times the amount of fat that cow milk does. The fat in its mother's milk helps sustain the calf during the long periods between feedings. The high fat content also helps the young giraffe grow quickly.

Baby giraffes sit in tall grass to shade themselves from the heat of the Sun.

Giraffe
Facts

What appears to be a giraffe's "knee" is actually more like a human's wrist.

Only female giraffes have tufts of fur on the tops of their horns. Males' horns are bald.

Infant giraffes often can run within 1 hour of their birth.

Development

Giraffe mothers give birth standing up. A calf's front feet and head emerge first. The calf falls about 6.5 feet (2 m) to the ground. Compared to its height, a newborn calf's neck is fairly short. In their first few months, calves may grow as much as 9 inches (23 cm) each week. The hair of newborns is soft and short, and their horns lie pressed against their heads. In a short time, however, the horns stand up.

Life can be quite dangerous for young giraffes. Lions, leopards, hyenas, crocodiles, and wild dogs take many calves. Three out of four young giraffes die before they are 1 year old.

Although a calf will nurse for about 9 months, it will feed on leaves once it is about 1 month old. At 6 months, a young giraffe may be almost 10 feet (3 m) tall. By the time it reaches 2 years of age, the young giraffe will become completely independent.

After 2 years of age, a giraffe's growth rate decreases. By the age of 5, female giraffes reach their adult height. Male giraffes continue to grow until they are about 7 years old.

At birth, the infant giraffe's fall to the ground forces it to take a big breath.

Habitat

In nature, giraffes live mainly in Central and Southern Africa. Only certain areas, such as grasslands and open woodlands, make good giraffe habitats. There must be enough trees and bushes for the animals to eat. The plant life cannot be so dense, however, that it blocks a giraffe's view of predators. Females without young and males tend to live in more heavily forested areas. Females with young live in more open areas. In such areas, it is easier for mother giraffes to spot danger and protect their young.

Giraffes can go for several days without water. This allows them to live in dry areas that are not suitable for many other African animals. It also allows giraffes to travel farther in search of good grazing areas.

Organizing the Grasslands and Open Woodlands

Earth is home to millions of different **organisms**, all of which have specific survival needs. These organisms rely on their environment, or the place where they live, for their survival. All plants and animals have relationships with their environment. They interact with the environment itself, as well as the other plants and animals within the environment. These interactions create **ecosystems**.

Ecosystems can be broken down into levels of organization. These levels range from a single plant or animal to many species of plants and animals living together in an area.

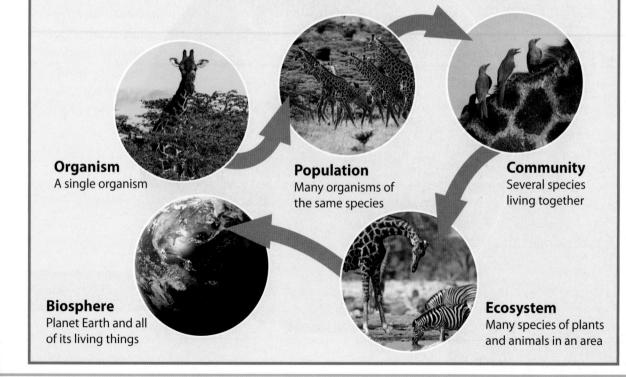

Organism
A single organism

Population
Many organisms of the same species

Community
Several species living together

Biosphere
Planet Earth and all of its living things

Ecosystem
Many species of plants and animals in an area

The seeds of the kameeldoring tree, a type of acacia, begin to grow only after passing through a giraffe's digestive system.

Giraffes once lived all across Southern Africa in arid grassland regions. Now they are found only in certain areas.

The word *giraffe* comes from an Arabic word meaning "one that walks very fast."

Large numbers of giraffes live in the East African country of Kenya.

Range

A giraffe's **home range** can be as small as 2 square miles (5 square kilometers) and as large as 260 square miles (675 sq. km). The home range of a female giraffe averages about 24 square miles (62 sq. km). Male home ranges average about 33 square miles (86 sq. km). Males have larger home ranges because they travel farther in search of females to mate with. Males also spend more time in forested areas that are dangerous for a female with a calf. These areas may contain hidden predators.

Giraffes once lived across what is now the Sahara Desert and in areas of North Africa near the Mediterranean Sea. Today, they are found only south of the Sahara. In Central Africa, most giraffes live in eastern regions. Only a few groups live in the west, where the forests tend to be denser. Like many other species, giraffes are decreasing in number because their natural habitat is disappearing as a result of human activities.

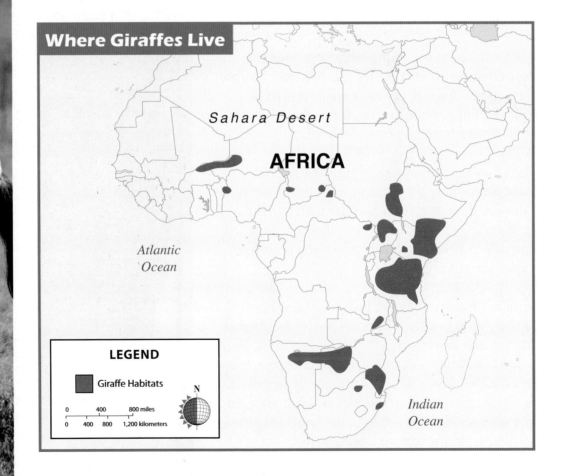

Where Giraffes Live

Sahara Desert

AFRICA

Atlantic Ocean

Indian Ocean

LEGEND

Giraffe Habitats

N

| 0 | 400 | 800 miles |
| 0 | 400 | 800 | 1,200 kilometers |

Movement

The giraffe has only two ways of moving from one place to another. It either walks or gallops. During the day, when they do most of their eating, giraffes walk quite slowly. They travel only about 0.1 miles (0.2 km) per hour. Lone males tend to travel farther and faster.

A giraffe can travel at a gallop for long distances without getting tired. The record running speed of this animal is 35 miles (55 km) per hour. Male giraffes will chase off other males at a gallop.

Giraffes will gallop away when they are being chased. Sometimes, they gallop away from things that frighten them. Unfamiliar sights and sounds, like airplanes flying overhead, will cause giraffes to stampede.

Giraffes can become familiar with situations that occur often, however. Giraffes that live near Nairobi International Airport in Kenya are now used to airplanes. They do not even look up when the planes fly overhead.

When they were often shot by hunters, giraffes would gallop away if a person came close. Today, in protected areas, giraffes familiar with tourists are much less likely to gallop off when a person approaches. This is especially true if the person is in a vehicle.

A giraffe's feet are about 12 inches (30 cm) long by 9 inches (23 cm) wide. The hoofs are wedge shaped. They get narrower toward the back of the foot. Prints made by the front hoofs are usually wider than those from the back hoofs. The prints made by females and young are narrower than those of an adult male. In older animals, the two halves of the hoofs may have spread apart more, making a wider print.

When a giraffe is walking, it can cover as much as 15 feet (4.6 m) with one stride.

Giraffes in zoos and reserves are used to people. They may allow people to come close.

Diet

The giraffe is an herbivore, which means that it feeds on plants. Herbivores tend to spend much of their time eating in order to get enough nutrients to live. In addition, since giraffes are large animals, they need a great deal of food to survive. Giraffes spend more time eating than doing any other activity. A giraffe spends about 16 to 20 hours each day feeding.

Giraffes are browsers. They eat parts of trees and shrubs. Other herbivores are grazers, which means they eat grass. An adult giraffe eats up to 74 pounds (34 kg) of leaves in a day.

A giraffe's favorite food is the leaves from thorny acacia trees and bushes. Giraffes in nature will also eat more than 100 other types of plants. Giraffes usually eat the leaves and small twigs from large shrubs, trees, and vines. They sometimes eat bark, thorns, flowers, and fruits. To get the minerals they need, giraffes will also eat salt or salty soil. Giraffes have even been seen eating meat off dead animals, but this is not common.

Giraffes often share their habitat with antelopes. When giraffes browse on trees, they eat above the level that antelopes can reach. Antelopes can eat leaves as high as 7 feet (2.1 m) above the ground. Giraffes eat from that point up to about 16 feet (4.8 m).

Giraffes get most of the water they need from the foods they eat. This helps them survive for long periods without drinking water. Giraffes also lick the morning dew off plants.

To drink water, a giraffe must lower its head all the way down to the ground. To do this, it must either bend its knees forward or spread its front legs wide apart. It will remain bent down drinking for short periods, usually 20 to 60 seconds.

Giraffe
Facts

A giraffe brings up food from its stomach to chew again. A giraffe's neck is so long that food can be seen moving up its throat and into its mouth.

At least one giraffe usually watches for predators while others are drinking.

A food cycle shows how energy, in the form of food, is passed from one living thing to another. Giraffes get energy by eating plants. In turn, giraffes provide energy to other animals in their environment. In the diagram below, the arrows show the flow of energy from one living thing to the next through a **food web**.

Producers
Plants use sunlight to produce food energy. Herbivores and omnivores, which eat both plants and animals, get energy from plants.

Primary Consumers
Giraffes prefer the leaves of acacia trees and bushes, but they will eat many different plant species to get the food energy they need.

Secondary Consumers
Lions prey on adult giraffes. Cheetahs, hyenas, leopards, and crocodiles hunt and eat young giraffes. A dead giraffe is a source of food for many **scavengers**.

Parasites

Living giraffes provide food and a home for many parasites, including about 30 species of ticks. Oxpeckers, which can sometimes be seen on a giraffe's back, are birds that feed on the parasites living on a giraffe's skin.

Decomposers

When a giraffe dies, decomposers break down its body. This adds nutrients to the soil, helping trees and other plants to grow.

•Debate•
Take a Stand
•Research•

Should human settlements and development be banned in areas where giraffes live?

In some African countries, giraffes browse close to farmland and villages. In others, they are restricted to reserves that are patrolled by guards. Land, plants, and water are valuable both to giraffes and to people.

FOR

1. Humans sometimes cut down the very trees and other plants that giraffes depend on as their food source. The giraffes do not have enough to eat.
2. Giraffes are used to roaming freely over vast areas. Roads, villages, and farms interfere with this movement. Giraffes cannot breed easily with animals from other herds.

AGAINST

1. Many people living in the same areas as giraffes have few ways to make money. Reserving land strictly for giraffes does not allow these people to grow crops for their families and to sell in markets.
2. Tourists like to see giraffes and spend in poor areas that have them. Allowing development means that tourist hotels and restaurants can be built. Residents who depend on the tourist industry will make sure giraffes thrive.

In battles over mating or territory, giraffes slam their necks against their opponents.

Animals on the Brink

Competition

G iraffes tend to ignore other species that browse or graze with them. Animals such as zebras and wildebeests feed near giraffes. They benefit from the giraffes' good eyesight and height, which allow giraffes to see possible predators from far away.

Sometimes food is scarce, especially during the dry season. Giraffes' long necks give them an advantage over shorter grazing animals. They can reach the higher leaves on trees. Only elephants can reach as high. Giraffes also eat the leaves from low bushes.

Male giraffes sometimes fight with each other. Most fights are to determine which male is dominant or which one will mate with a female. Males fight with their necks, heads, and horns in a type of fighting called necking. Their heads are extremely large and heavy. A giraffe's head alone can weigh more than 55 pounds (25 kg) and be 27 inches (68.6 cm) long.

During a fight, one giraffe will lower its head and swing it at the other giraffe. The other giraffe will try to move out of the way and then will swing back. The giraffes try to hit each other with their horns. Because their horns are blunt, these matches appear to be harmless. In very rare cases, however, they result in a giraffe's being seriously injured or killed. Even in very serious necking matches, the giraffes never bite or kick each other.

From an Expert

"Each year of study revealed the fascinating adaptations that have allowed giraffes to survive for millions of years."
Bristol Foster

Bristol Foster is a wildlife scientist who has spent many years studying giraffes in Nairobi National Park in Kenya. He taught at the University of Nairobi. His 1976 study of mother and baby giraffes, *The Giraffe: Its Biology, Behavior, and Ecology*, remains a valuable book for people interested in giraffes.

Giraffes with Other Animals

The adult giraffe has few enemies. Besides humans, lions are the giraffe's main predator. Lions attack and eat giraffes of all ages and sizes.

Going after a giraffe can be dangerous, even for a lion. Adult giraffes often kick out at lions when they or their young are attacked. There have been several reports of giraffes hurting lions by kicking them or by trampling them to death.

Cheetahs, hyenas, leopards, and even crocodiles may occasionally take down adult giraffes. However, they more often attack small giraffes, which are easier to capture. A full-grown giraffe has little to fear from these predators.

Humans have proven to be a dangerous enemy. They have hunted giraffes and destroyed large parts of their habitat. Diseases from cattle and other livestock raised by farmers have infected giraffes.

Two species of birds, the red-billed oxpecker and the yellow-billed oxpecker, will often ride on giraffes. While searching for ticks on the giraffes, the birds remove dirt and dry skin. These birds also remove maggots from any wounds. They alert giraffes to predators by flying away when alarmed.

Giraffes use their big, powerful feet to fight off predators.

Giraffe
Facts

Unlike horses, giraffes can reach almost any part of their body with their tail. This helps them whisk away pests.

Other animals take advantage of the giraffe's keen sight and hearing. They graze safely, knowing the giraffe is on the watch for predators.

Folklore

Throughout history, giraffes have been described as having features that combine those of other animals. The ancient Romans thought the giraffe looked like a cross between a camel and a leopard. Its long neck and two-toed hoofs like a camel and its spots like a leopard gave the Romans this idea. In the first century AD, a giraffe was described as a combination of a horse, an ox, and a camel. In 1022, an Arab geographer suggested that giraffes were produced when male panthers mated with female camels. Another scholar said giraffes were produced by a female camel, a male hyena, and a cow.

Recently, the giraffe has been seen as a symbol of goodness. Ann Medlock started the Giraffe Project in 1984. The project honors people who "stick their necks out" to help other people. The organization sees the giraffe as a perfect role model for several reasons. It has a big heart. It is an herbivore, so it does not eat other creatures. It is often silent but has the strength to fight a lion if necessary.

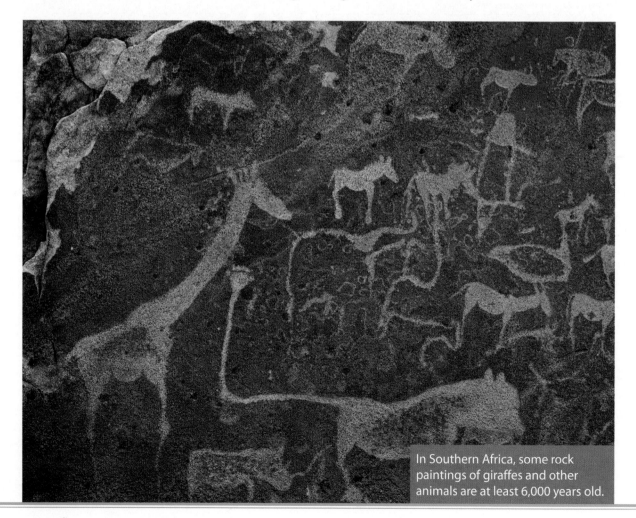

In Southern Africa, some rock paintings of giraffes and other animals are at least 6,000 years old.

Myth	**VS**	Fact
A giraffe's front legs are much longer than its back legs.		The slope of a giraffe's back makes its front legs appear much longer than its back legs. In fact, all four of its legs are about the same length. Its front legs are only 10 percent longer than its back legs.
Giraffes are gentle and harmless.		Although giraffes rarely attack other animals, they will defend themselves when threatened. Giraffes kick with enormous power. They have badly hurt attacking lions, cheetahs, and other animals by kicking them in the head.
Giraffes always sleep standing up.		Although giraffes occasionally sleep standing up, they usually lie down. To sleep deeply, a giraffe bends its head back alongside its body and rests it on the ground. During one night, an adult giraffe might do this five times, sleeping for about three or four minutes each time.

Giraffes capture the imagination of artists all over the world.

Giraffes were found throughout Africa 10,000 years ago. Later, giraffes became **extinct** in North Africa as the climate changed and most of the area became a desert. Giraffes became extinct in Egypt about 4,000 years ago and in Morocco about 1,400 years ago.

Thousands of giraffes were shot by early European hunters, settlers, and explorers in Africa. The giraffe became a special target for "big game" hunters. These hunters often wrote about their exploits. They mentioned chasing the giraffe as being the best part of the hunt. They admired its unusual and distinctive way of galloping. Some hunters, however, questioned how "sporting" it was to shoot a giraffe. Frederick Vaughan Kirby, a British hunter, wrote in 1896, "One can scarcely consider it an elevating form of sport . . . for it calls forth neither endurance, courage, nor extraordinary skill on the part of the hunter." He thought that all giraffe hunting should be stopped or the animals would be hunted to extinction.

For hunters with guns, a giraffe is an easy target.

In 1999, the International Union for Conservation of Nature (IUCN) estimated that there were more than 140,000 giraffes in Central and Southern Africa. This included almost 50,000 giraffes living in and around protected areas.

In the past two decades, however, the number of giraffes living in Africa has dropped. Today, scientists estimate that only about 80,000 animals survive in nature. Villages and farms have taken over much of their traditional browsing land.

Poachers have been harvesting giraffes illegally in protected reserves. In areas where hunting is legal, people pay businesses that organize safaris between $1,800 and $3,800 to join a safari where they can shoot a giraffe. The hunters often take the head or skin as a trophy, leaving behind the meat. Sometimes, they want only a photo of themselves with the dead giraffe.

GIRAFFE POPULATIONS	
Angolan giraffe	20,000
Cape giraffe	12,000
Kordofan giraffe	3,000
Masai giraffe	40,000
Nigerian giraffe	250
Nubian giraffe	250
Reticulated giraffe	5,000
Rothschild's giraffe	670
Thornicroft's giraffe	1,500

Take a Stand
· Debate ·
· Research ·

Should hunters be allowed to shoot giraffes?

Although some African countries prohibit giraffe hunting, others sell licenses to hunt the animal. Farmers are sometimes permitted to shoot giraffes that are damaging their crops or fences. Although very few giraffes are taken this way, many people feel that all hunting of giraffes should be stopped.

FOR

1. Money raised from licenses can be used for conservation projects to help giraffes.
2. The few giraffes taken in this way may not affect the population, especially in areas where the giraffe population is stable or increasing.

AGAINST

1. Very little money is raised through licensing compared to that raised by tourism in the wildlife parks.
2. Hunting causes the decline of the giraffe species. It reduces the number of animals available for breeding.

Each year, thousands of people visit Giraffe Manor in Kenya to see the giraffes that have been given a safe home there.

Animals on the Brink

Saving the Giraffe

In the early 1970s, a group of 130 Rothschild's giraffes living on a large cattle ranch in western Kenya were in trouble. The government decided to divide the ranch into small plots of land and move people into the area. This would leave no room for the giraffes.

Betty and Jock Leslie-Melville founded the African Fund for Endangered Wildlife to raise money to move the giraffes. Betty was an American living in Nairobi, Kenya, and her husband, Jock, was a Kenyan citizen originally from Great Britain. With their help, four groups of giraffes were relocated to national parks where they could live more safely.

Betty and Jock also moved some young Rothschild's giraffes to their home in Nairobi. Now called Giraffe Manor, the home is an educational center open to the public. The African Fund for Endangered Wildlife runs Giraffe Manor. Every year, nearly 62,000 African schoolchildren visit the center free of charge to learn about animal conservation.

The giraffes living at Giraffe Manor are very comfortable around people. The lands surrounding Giraffe Manor are protected. The giraffe sanctuary now includes more than 100 acres (40.5 hectares). After Jock's death in the mid-1980s, Betty continued working, with her son, to protect giraffes. She was awarded a Safari Planet Earth Award in 1994 for her efforts.

Plans to relocate more Rothschild's giraffes are under way. One goal is to help the individuals of different groups breed with one another. This helps the animals remain healthy by seeing that more matings between unrelated giraffes take place.

"Today most of the countries in Africa protect their giraffes by laws which punish all poachers. . . . . Eventually, because of human population pressures, the giraffe will likely be restricted to national parks and game reserves in Africa."
Anne Innis Dagg

The author of 18 books, Anne Innis Dagg is a zoologist, animal rights activist, and wildlife photographer. She has also studied giraffe behavior and ecology in nature in Africa, as well as the heredity and behavior of zoo giraffes.

Back from the Brink

The IUCN now classifies the entire giraffe species as being of "least concern." This means that most giraffe subspecies are not considered to be **endangered**. However, if current programs to protect giraffes are stopped, these giraffes could become endangered in just a few years. The biggest threats to giraffes today are poaching and loss of habitat as a result of settlements and civil unrest.

The IUCN considers the Angolan and Cape giraffe populations to be stable. Populations of other giraffe species, however, are decreasing steadily. For example, Rothschild's giraffes were declared endangered in 2010. The Nigerian giraffe is also considered endangered.

In the northern and western parts of the giraffe's range, population decreases are due mainly to poaching. In these areas, giraffes live in small, scattered populations. In the eastern part of Central Africa and in Southern Africa, giraffes are widespread. In the southern parts of their range, giraffe numbers are increasing due to effective protection provided by parks, reserves, and private landowners.

The Giraffe Conservation Foundation works to find more land for giraffes to roam freely and to keep current protected areas safe. It also researches today's giraffe populations to discover how many giraffes there are and how healthy they are. It hopes to find ways to conserve and manage herds. For more information on the work of the Giraffe Conservation Foundation, contact:

Giraffe Conservation Foundation UK
26 Grasmere Road
Purley, Surrey, England CR8 1DU

Giraffe Conservation Foundation Africa
P.O. Box 86099
Eros, Namibia

Fewer than 700 Rothschild's giraffes live in reserves and on private land in Africa.

Activity

Debating helps people think about ideas thoughtfully and carefully. When people debate, two sides take a different viewpoint on a subject. Each side takes turns presenting arguments to support its view.

Use the Take a Stand sections found throughout this book as a starting point for debate topics. Organize your friends or classmates into two teams. One team will argue in favor of the topic, and the other will argue against. Each team should research the issue thoroughly using reliable sources of information, including books, scientific journals, and trustworthy websites. Take notes of important facts that support your side of the debate. Prepare your argument using these facts to support your opinion.

During the debate, the members of each team are given a set amount of time to make their arguments. The team arguing the For side goes first. They have five minutes to present their case. All members of the team should participate equally. Then, the team arguing the Against side presents its arguments. Each team should take notes of the main points the other team argues.

After both teams have made their arguments, they get three minutes to prepare their rebuttals. Teams review their notes from the previous round. The teams focus on trying to disprove each of the main points made by the other team using solid facts. Each team gets three minutes to make its rebuttal. The team arguing the Against side goes first. Students and teachers watching the debate serve as judges. They should try to judge the debate fairly using a standard score sheet, such as the example below.

Criteria	Rate: 1-10	Sample Comments
1. Were the arguments well organized?	8	logical arguments, easy to follow
2. Did team members participate equally?	9	divided time evenly between members
3. Did team members speak loudly and clearly?	3	some members were difficult to hear
4. Were rebuttals specific to the other team's arguments?	6	rebuttals were specific, more facts needed
5. Was respect shown for the other team?	10	all members showed respect to the other team

Quiz

2. How fast can a giraffe run?

3. What is the giraffe's closest relative?

1. Why are giraffes' tongues purple?

5. How tall is a baby giraffe when it is born?

6. How do giraffes sleep?

4. What is a giraffe's favorite food?

8. Which subspecies of giraffes are considered endangered?

9. Which animals prey on giraffes?

7. Which birds clean giraffes' skin?

10. How do male giraffes fight?

Answers:
1. to prevent sunburn 2. up to 35 miles (55 km) per hour 3. the okapi 4. leaves from acacia trees and bushes 5. about 6 feet (1.8 m) tall 6. lying down with their heads on the ground 7. the red-billed oxpecker and the yellow-billed oxpecker 8. the Rothschild's giraffe and the Nigerian giraffe 9. lions, cheetahs, hyenas, leopards, and crocodiles 10. by necking, which is fighting with their necks, heads, and horns

adaptations: changes made to fit into a certain environment

cartilage: an elastic tissue that sometimes changes to bone

dominance: the state of having control and authority

ecosystems: communities of living things and resources

endangered: a type of plant or animal that exists in such small numbers that it is in danger of no longer surviving in the world or in a certain area

extinct: no longer surviving in the world or in a certain area

food web: connecting food chains that show how energy flows from one organism to another through diet

gestation period: the length of time a female is pregnant with young

habitat: the place where animals live, grow, and raise their young

heat: the period of time during which a female giraffe is ready and willing to mate with a male giraffe

home range: the entire area in which a giraffe and its family lives

mammals: warm-blooded animals that have hair or fur and nurse their young

necking: when two giraffes hit each other repeatedly with their heads

nursing: when a mammal provides its young with mother's milk

organisms: forms of life

poachers: people who kill an animal illegally

predators: animals that live by hunting other animals for food

prehensile: adapted for gripping objects, especially by wrapping around them

scavengers: animals that eat dead animals that they have not killed

species: groups of individuals with common characteristics

submissive: docile toward, or giving in to, another animal or human

tannins: yellow or brown substances in some plants that taste bitter

ultraviolet: a kind of light ray within sunlight

Index

Log on to www.av2books.com

AV² by Weigl brings you media enhanced books that support active learning. Go to www.av2books.com, and enter the special code found on page 2 of this book. You will gain access to enriched and enhanced content that supplements and complements this book. Content includes video, audio, weblinks, quizzes, a slide show, and activities.

AV² Online Navigation

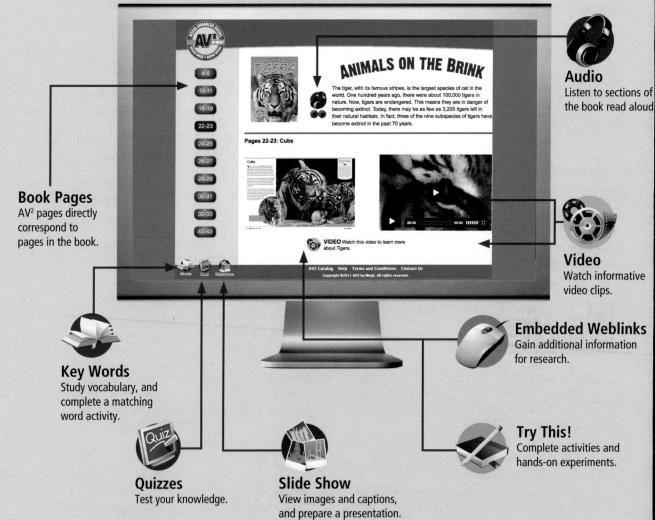

Book Pages
AV² pages directly correspond to pages in the book.

Audio
Listen to sections of the book read aloud

Video
Watch informative video clips.

Key Words
Study vocabulary, and complete a matching word activity.

Embedded Weblinks
Gain additional information for research.

Quizzes
Test your knowledge.

Slide Show
View images and captions, and prepare a presentation.

Try This!
Complete activities and hands-on experiments.

AV² was built to bridge the gap between print and digital. We encourage you to tell us what you like and what you want to see in the future.

Sign up to be an AV² Ambassador at www.av2books.com/ambassador.

Due to the dynamic nature of the Internet, some of the URLs and activities provided as part of AV² by Weigl may have changed or ceased to exist. AV² by Weigl accepts no responsibility for any such changes. All media enhanced books are regularly monitored to update addresses and sites in a timely manner. Contact AV² by Weigl at 1-866-649-3445 or av2books@weigl.com with any questions, comments, or feedback.